I0816947

WEIRD WORLD

WEIRD EXPERIMENTS

BY A. W. BUCKEY

Core Library

An Imprint of Abdo Publishing
abdobooks.com

Cover image: One experiment found evidence that driving tiny cars reduces stress in rats.

abdobooks.com

Published by Abdo Publishing, a division of ABDO, PO Box 398166, Minneapolis, Minnesota 55439.
Copyright © 2026 by Abdo Consulting Group, Inc. International copyrights reserved in all countries. No part of this book may be reproduced in any form without written permission from the publisher. Core Library™ is a trademark and logo of Abdo Publishing.

Printed in the United States of America, North Mankato, Minnesota.
102025
012026

Cover Photo: Ryan M. Kelly/AFP/Getty Images
Interior Photos: Cover Images/ZUMA Press/Newscom, 4–5; Shutterstock Images, 7, 18–19, 32, 39 (fly), 39 (monkey), 39 (mouse), 39 (spider); Kirn Vintage Stock/Archive Photos/Getty Images, 10–11, 43; Ryan M. Kelly/AFP/Getty Images, 12; Fernando Calmon/Shutterstock Images, 15; Danny Ye/Shutterstock Images, 16; Jordi Vidal/Getty Images Entertainment/Getty Images, 20; William Taufic/The Image Bank/Getty Images, 24–25, 45; Bob Riha Jr./Archive Photos/Getty Images, 27; Bernard Friel/Education Images/Universal Images Group/Getty Images, 28; Red Line Editorial, 31; NASA, 34–35; Eye of Science/Science Source, 37; Sovfoto/Universal Images Group/Getty Images, 39 (dog); Lauren Suryanata/Shutterstock Images, 39 (tortoise); NOAA, 39 (fish)

Editor: Riley Madsen
Series Designer: Marley Richmond

Library of Congress Control Number: 2025939321

Publisher's Cataloging-in-Publication Data

Names: Buckey, A. W., author.
Title: Weird experiments / by A. W. Buckey
Description: Minneapolis, Minnesota: Abdo Publishing, 2026 | Series: Weird world | Includes online resources and index.
Identifiers: ISBN 9781098298470 (lib. bdg.) | ISBN 9798384932277 (ebook)
Subjects: LCSH: Oddities--Juvenile literature. | Experiments--Juvenile literature. | Science--Experiments--Juvenile literature. | Science projects--Juvenile literature. | Discoveries in science--History--Juvenile literature. | Curiosities and wonders--Juvenile literature.
Classification: DDC 507.8--dc23

CONTENTS

CHAPTER ONE

THE WOOLLY MOUSE

In March 2025, scientists at Colossal Biosciences, headquartered in Dallas, Texas, made a big announcement. They had created a new type of mouse. It was golden brown, fluffy, and very cute. Unlike most mice, the new mouse did not have a sleek coat. Instead, its hair stood up in tufts. This hair was three times longer than an average mouse's fur.

That wasn't the only special thing about this mouse. Scientists had altered its DNA. DNA is the material in a living thing's cells that tells the cells

In total, scientists altered eight genes to produce the woolly mouse, *left*. The mouse on the right is a normal mouse.

what to become and how to behave. A mouse's DNA is responsible for traits such as fur color, body size, and tail length. The scientists at Colossal had changed the new mouse's DNA to give it long, wavy fur. They also changed a fat-storing gene.

These changes had a purpose. The goal was to make a mouse that shared traits with an animal that had disappeared from Earth about 4,000 years ago. The scientists wanted a mouse that was like a woolly mammoth.

Woolly mammoths were large mammals similar to elephants. They lived in the northernmost parts of Earth. Scientists know what the mammoths were like based on

TRANSGENIC MICE

Mice that have changes made to their genes are called *transgenic*. Scientists have been making transgenic mice since 1980. The process has several steps. First, researchers change mouse DNA. They put the DNA inside a mouse egg. They then implant the egg inside a female mouse. The female mouse gives birth to a transgenic baby. Some transgenic mice glow in the dark. Others help with disease research.

Woolly mammoths and humans shared Earth for about 20,000 years before woolly mammoths went extinct.

fossils and the DNA found inside them. Colossal wants to bring the woolly mammoth back to Earth. The company thinks that someday, it might be able to create elephants with the mammoth's fur coat and thick layer of fat. But for now, the company is practicing on the smaller woolly mouse.

WHAT ARE EXPERIMENTS?

An experiment is a test. Experiments start with questions about the universe. Why do some plants grow

EUREKA!

People have been coming up with weird experiments for thousands of years. Archimedes was a scientist and inventor in ancient Greece. In one story, Archimedes was trying to help a king find the volume of his crown. He was thinking about the problem in his bathtub. Suddenly, he realized that he could measure the volume of objects placed in water. All he had to do was see how much the water rose in the container when the object was added. Archimedes ran through the streets shouting, "Eureka!" The word means "I have found it!" in Greek.

faster than others? How do animals learn? What happens to objects in space? Then the experimenter comes up with a hypothesis. That's an idea that can be tested. An experiment finds a way to test the hypothesis. Then experimenters share their results. This allows other people to try the experiment.

Experiments help people learn about the world. New medicines, products, and technologies all rely on experiments. But the universe is a weird place. And some people ask weird questions about it.

STRAIGHT TO THE SOURCE

Mice are often used in animal research and in experiments of many kinds. This page from the European Animal Research Association explains some of the reasons that scientists do research with mice:

> *Few mammals have been as closely studied as the mouse and its genetic map (genome) has been fully sequenced, which means that its genes can be switched on and off to study their effects. . . . Mice have short lifespans (2–3 years), making them ideal for looking at the progression of diseases that may otherwise take years to develop and study in humans. . . . Mice are quick and easy to breed. . . . This means that sufficient numbers of mice needed for research are available.*

Source: "Mice and Animal Research." *European Animal Research Association*, n.d., eara.eu. Accessed 2 May 2025.

BACK IT UP

The author of this passage is using evidence to support a point. Write a paragraph describing the point the author is making. Then write down two or three pieces of evidence the author uses to make the point.

CHAPTER TWO

WEIRD EXPERIMENTS ON ANIMALS

Many experiments involve animals. Some experiments aim to test hypotheses about the animals themselves. Others are designed to help medical researchers learn more about diseases that affect humans and how to treat them. Some animal experiments can seem pretty weird.

Rats are smart animals. They can use tools and solve problems. But the scientists at the University

Professional scientists follow ethical guidelines to minimize animal suffering when using animals in experiments.

Researchers found that rats raised in more natural environments were better drivers than rats raised in laboratories.

of Richmond in Virginia had a question. They wanted to know if rats could learn to drive. The scientists hypothesized that it was possible.

To test their hypothesis, the scientists made rat-sized cars. They called them Rat-Operated Vehicles (ROVs). Atop the ROVs were plastic food jars. On the bottom was a set of wheels. The wheels were connected to copper wire. The rats stood on a metal floor and learned to touch metal steering bars. Touching the bars made the wheels spin. Rats who learned to drive earned pieces of sugary cereal as a reward. The rats got better at driving over time. They learned to drive routes they had never tried before.

After the rats learned to drive, the scientists collected their poop. They tested the poop for clues about the rats' feelings. Hormones are chemicals that carry messages throughout the body. They can come out in poop. The scientists found that driving rats

ARTISTIC PIGEONS

A weird study found that pigeons have an eye for art. In 1995, scientists in Japan put groups of pigeons in front of screens. The screens displayed paintings by various artists. The pigeons were rewarded with seeds for pecking in response to certain artists. Soon, they could tell Monet and Picasso paintings apart. They even learned to tell the difference between painting styles.

had lower stress hormones. They also had more of a hormone that decreases stress.

The scientists wanted to know if simply riding in a car would help rats de-stress. They designed another experiment. This time, they put rats in the ROVs as passengers. The researchers tested these rats' poop too. It did not have as much of the de-stressing hormone in it. The scientists think that rats enjoy driving more than riding. This could be because learning new things may be rewarding for rats.

Humans and rats are much alike. Rat brains and human brains have many of the same parts. Studying rats can reveal things about humans. The University of Richmond scientists hope their rat research can help people. They study people with mental health conditions such as depression. Depression often causes low energy and sad moods. The condition can make it difficult for a person to de-stress. Scientists wonder whether results from rat experiments can help doctors design new treatments for people with depression.

ALLIGATORS ON GAS

Animals do not use language the same way humans do. But animals do communicate in a variety of ways. They use smells, movements, colors, and sounds to send messages. Scientists study these communication methods. Sometimes they find weird ways to do it.

Many birds communicate with their voices. When a bird wants to show how big it is, it uses resonance. Resonance is one way that many animals, including humans, produce sounds. These animals have parts that vibrate as air passes over them. This allows them

Different species of birds can have remarkably different birdsongs.

Chinese alligators are a distinct species of alligator that are smaller than American alligators.

to produce a wide range of sounds. Birds with full, resonant voices sound bigger than they really are. They may use resonance to impress mates or warn predators to stay away.

Alligators and birds are distant relatives. Dinosaurs are their common ancestors. Alligators make noises called bellows. Scientists wondered how alligators made bellows. It was possible that they used resonance. But it was also possible that they used another method, such as rubbing or striking internal organs.

In 2015, researchers at Kyoto University in Japan decided to find out. They put Chinese alligators in a tank with water and air. The alligators came up to breathe the oxygen in the air. The researchers recorded the alligators' bellows. They then put the alligators in a tank with water, oxygen, and helium. Helium is a gas. It is less dense than air. When people breathe in helium, their voices get high and squeaky. This is because helium changes resonance. When the alligators breathed in helium, their bellows got higher too. This was proof that these animals used resonance.

THE IG NOBEL PRIZE

The alligator helium experiment won an Ig Nobel Prize. This is an award for strange and silly science experiments. The prize's name is a play on the famous Nobel Prize and on the word *ignoble*, which means "dishonorable." Like the Nobel Prize, the Ig Nobel Prize is given yearly. The prize goes to research that seems weird but has an important purpose.

WEIRD EXPERIMENTS ON PLANTS

In 1962, Indian botanist Dr. T. C. Singh asked a weird question. He wondered if music could help plants grow. Plants have no ears. They cannot hear the way animals and humans can. But Singh still thought music could make a difference. He grew plants and played music for them. He played classical Western and Indian music. Singh found that plants that spent time in the presence of music grew taller. They also weighed more.

Although plants cannot hear the way humans can, sound vibrations may have an effect on plants.

In June 2022, a string quartet performed a concert for an audience of plants.

Since then, many people have tried playing music for plants. They have played classical music and rock music for bok choy cabbage. They have tried loud, intense metal music. A theater in Italy put on a concert just for plants. There are even musical albums intended to be played to plants.

Researchers have considered explanations for why plants seem to respond to music. Sounds such as music travel as vibrations in the air. These vibrations reach nearby plants. They move the plants' cells.

One explanation says that these movements may help plants better carry nutrients.

PLANT THOUGHTS AND PLANT TALK

Dr. Singh's music experiments with plants made people wonder what other unusual factors could affect plants. Cleve Backster decided to find out. Backster was not a scientist. He worked for the US military. Later, he joined the Central Intelligence Agency (CIA). The CIA hires and trains spies.

Backster worked as a polygraph machine expert. The polygraph machine is sometimes called a lie detector test. Electrodes connect the machine to a person.

THE MUSICAL TASTE OF YEAST AND BACTERIA

Yeast and bacteria are simple life-forms. Each individual consists of only a single cell. But even these simple living things may react to music. A 2015 study played music for bacteria and yeast. Most of the life-forms grew more when music was played.

THE COUNTING VENUS FLYTRAP

Plants do not think the way humans do. But some plants do have ways of counting. The traps on Venus flytraps have sensors. They look like little hairs. Touching the hairs releases chemicals. The chemicals close the trap. In 2016, a team of scientists in Germany tested what made the plant's trap close. It found that the trap closed only after the hairs were touched more than once. This ability may help the plant make sure there is prey in the trap before closing.

The machine measures things such as the person's heart rate and blood pressure. When a person gets nervous, his heart rate and blood pressure increase. Some consider using polygraph machines to be a reliable way of detecting when someone is lying.

Backster wondered if plants get nervous too. In 1966, he used the machine on a houseplant in his office. He attached electrodes to the plant. His plan was to burn one of its leaves and read the results on the polygraph. As he thought about burning the leaf, the polygraph showed signs of stress in the plant. Backster was shocked. He concluded that the plant had read his mind. He thought it sensed his plan to burn it and became distressed.

Backster did many more experiments on plants. But his results weren't real. Other people have tried the same experiments. They have not seen the same polygraph movements. This is a clue that his experiments were not well designed. Good experiments should be repeatable.

EXPLORE ONLINE

Chapter Three explains how playing music may help plants grow taller. This website explains how people can try this experiment for themselves. How does it help you understand the scientific process? Would you try this experiment at home? Why or why not?

DOES MUSIC AFFECT PLANT GROWTH

abdocorelibrary.com/weird-experiments

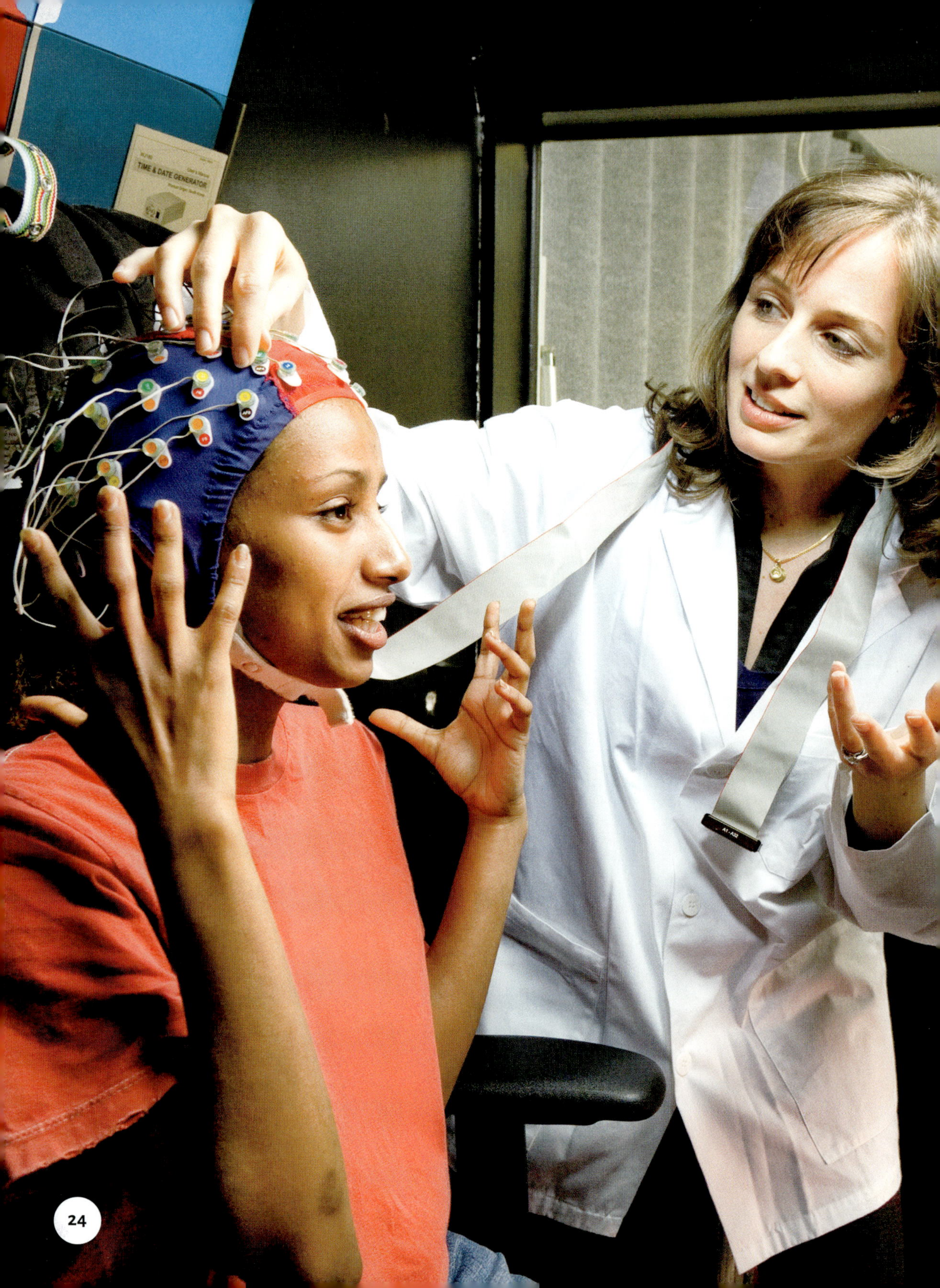
TIME & DATE GENERATOR

CHAPTER FOUR

WEIRD EXPERIMENTS ON PEOPLE

Many experiments seek to test hypotheses about people. These experiments may use people as experimental subjects. Some experiments try to learn more about the human mind. Others try to help doctors develop new treatments for diseases.

Some experiments on humans can be weird. But safety is the most important concern. Professional scientists carefully design experiments

In the United States, professional scientists must seek approval from an ethics committee before performing experiments on people.

that use human subjects. Experiments must follow guidelines set by the US government and by institutions such as universities. These guidelines aim to prevent abuse of human subjects and to minimize any risks subjects may face.

BIOSPHERE 2

Many people dream of a future in which humans live on planets other than Earth. But most planets are not suited for human life. Many planets lack the air that people need, and they may be too hot or too cold. For people to survive on such planets, they would need to build closed systems in which conditions for human life could be maintained. But people wonder what it would take to build such a system.

The Biosphere 2 experiment began as an attempt to test this question. In 1991, four men and four women went inside a large enclosed facility in Arizona called Biosphere 2. This facility was designed as a miniature version of Earth, which the experimenters referred to as

The Biosphere 2 facility was built in the desert outside Oracle, Arizona.

Biosphere 1. The facility contained areas modeled after ecosystems such as deserts and forests. Various plants and animals lived inside it along with the eight people. The facility was sealed to the outside world. Even the transfer of air between Biosphere 2 and the outside world was minimized. The eight people inside would do everything for themselves.

The experiment lasted two years. Life inside Biosphere 2 was tough. Farming was difficult. The residents sometimes lacked certain items. For example, they grew and made their own coffee. But they were only able to grow enough to have it every few weeks.

Visitors were allowed to enter Biosphere 2 starting in 2002.

After a few months, the people in Biosphere 2 had a very big problem. The facility didn't have enough oxygen. The people inside started to get sick. Eventually, they had to get oxygen from outside. Everyone in the experiment survived. They learned that building a closed world was harder than they had thought.

PERSUASION EXPERIMENTS

Human beings are social animals. People are drawn toward others. But when people are in groups, they can act in weird ways.

Solomon Asch was a famous psychologist. He studied the human mind. One of his interests was persuasion. He wanted to see how people influence each other. A 1951 study of his tested the persuasive power of conformity.

In the study, Asch put a group of people in a room. Researchers showed them pictures of vertical lines. Next to each line were three other lines. One line was the same length, one was shorter, and

TASTING TEA

More than 100 years ago, British scientist Muriel Bristol drank tea with milk. She said she could tell by taste whether the tea or the milk had been added to the cup first. Bristol's friend, mathematician Ronald Fisher, didn't believe her. He tested her by giving her eight cups of tea. Four were poured with milk first and four were poured with tea first. Fisher shuffled the cups and presented them to Bristol. If she truly couldn't tell which cup was which, there was only a small chance that she would make the correct selections. But she did. Fisher later used this experiment to demonstrate his ideas about how to design experiments in general.

one was longer. The differences in length were obvious. The group's task was to line up and answer one by one which two lines were the same length. The group performed this task 18 times in a row with different pictures.

But there was a catch. Only one person in the group was a real test subject. The others were actors. Asch and his coworkers told them what to say and do. When the participants lined up, the actors went first, and the real test subject went last. In the first six rounds, the actors gave

EXPECTING BOREDOM

People influence each other. But they also influence themselves. Expectations are powerful. One study examined the expectations of college students. Participating students were shown a video recording of a class lecture. Before some participants watched the video, experimenters made them anticipate that the lecture would be boring. All participants were then asked their opinion of the lecture. Participants who expected the lecture to be boring were more likely to say afterward that it was boring.

ASCH'S LINES

It was clear which two lines were the same length in Asch's experiment, but many participants disregarded what they saw due to social pressure. Why do you think social pressure caused people to give an answer they knew was wrong?

the right answers. Then they all started giving wrong answers. They said that two clearly different lines were the same length. The study subjects had to decide whether to agree or disagree. Disagreeing meant going against a group of seven other people. In Asch's study, most subjects gave a wrong answer at least once. The pressure to conform seemed to have made them doubt what they saw.

FURTHER EVIDENCE

Chapter Four discusses experiments on people. What was one of the main points of this chapter? What evidence is included to support this point? Read the article at the website below. Does the information on the website support the main point of the chapter? Does it present new evidence?

BIOSPHERE 2

abdocorelibrary.com/weird-experiments

Many psychology experiments use actors to create social situations that scientists want to study.

CHAPTER FIVE

WEIRD EXPERIMENTS IN SPACE

Living in space is not like living on Earth. Living things on Earth have developed traits to deal with gravity. This force affects every part of the body. Muscles must fight gravity to move the body. But on spaceships orbiting Earth, living things experience weightlessness. Space scientists are interested in how weightlessness affects living things.

KEN DAVE JEFF

Astronauts experience weightlessness on the International Space Station, a large spacecraft orbiting Earth.

Scientists have studied the effects of weightlessness in space in many ways. One study examined the effect of weightlessness on spiders. Golden silk spiders use gravity to help their sense of direction. This sense helps them weave their webs.

FEATHER AND HAMMER ON THE MOON

On Earth, heavier objects sometimes fall to the ground faster than lighter objects. For example, a feather falls slower than a hammer. However, this difference in falling speed is not due to the objects' masses. Instead, the feather falls slower than the hammer because it has a larger surface area than the hammer. This causes the feather to fall slower through air. In 1971, astronauts did an experiment on the mostly airless Moon. They dropped a feather and a hammer at the same time. The two objects fell at the same rate.

In 2011, a group of these spiders were carried into space. Researchers watched as they tried to spin their webs without the help of gravity. The spiders found another way to orient themselves. They used light as a guide instead. But the

Tardigrades are barely visible to the naked eye. Microscopes can give detailed views of these animals.

lack of gravity did affect the shapes of their webs. On Earth, the webs have a clear "up" and "down" side. In space, the difference was less clear.

TARDIGRADES IN A VACUUM

Outer space is a nearly perfect vacuum. Very few particles of matter float around in the vast void of space. Human beings have taken brief trips into this void outside of space shuttles and space stations. They must wear special suits to survive. But not all living things need such assistance.

Tardigrades are tiny animals about 0.04 inches (1 mm) long. They have serious survival skills. Tardigrades need water to thrive. But when there's no water, they can go into a kind of sleep. They slow down their bodies, staying dry and still. Tardigrades can live this way for years.

This behavior can keep tardigrades alive even in space. In 2007, a Russian mission sent 3,000 tardigrades into space. Some were sent into the vacuum. They were left there for ten days. Most of these tardigrades survived. They even gave birth to healthy baby tardigrades afterward.

TWINS IN SPACE

Space researchers think about whether humans could survive long space trips. Traveling to other planets in the solar system could take months and even years. Scientists want to prepare for the things that might happen to bodies in space. Studying twin astronauts is helping scientists do that.

ANIMALS IN SPACE

This is a partial list of the animals that have been to space and the years of their first flight. What do you notice about them? Why do you think scientists chose these animals?

Scott Kelly is an American astronaut. He is also an identical twin. Kelly and his twin brother Mark have almost identical DNA. In 2015, Scott Kelly went to space for an entire year. Mark Kelly is also an astronaut, but he stayed on Earth during this time. After Scott returned from space, scientists measured the differences in their bodies.

BED-REST STUDIES

Scientists have found a way to reproduce some of the effects of weightlessness on Earth. They study people who stay in bed for months. These people are paid to participate in bed-rest studies. They lie at an angle and do not get up. They eat, bathe, and even go to the bathroom in bed. Researchers study the effects on their bodies over time. This helps them learn about what long-term spaceflight might be like.

Scott's body had changed in space. For example, the shape of his eyeballs had slightly changed. This did not happen to Mark. In fact, there were thousands of small differences between the twins. Many of the changes to Scott's body disappeared after he came back to Earth.

STRAIGHT TO THE
SOURCE

Some people ask if it makes sense to send spiders into space. Others think that money spent on space experiments would be better used on Earth. The National Aeronautics and Space Administration's (NASA) point of view is that even weird space experiments can help humanity. It says:

> ***Research in space helps improve health on Earth, from understanding bone loss to developing vaccines to improving eye surgery.***
>
> ***Using the [International Space Station] and NASA satellites, we study Earth from space. NASA data helps predict the weather, monitor natural disasters like hurricanes and wildfires, and study long-term climate trends.***

Source: "Value of NASA." *NASA*, n.d., nasa.gov. Accessed 2 May 2025.

POINT OF VIEW

After reading this quote, read Chapter Five again. Do you think scientists and astronauts should experiment on plants, animals, and people in space? Why or why not? Use evidence to support your answer.

FAST FACTS

- Scientists design experiments to test questions about the universe. Some experiments have weird designs or produce weird results.
- The woolly mouse experiment involved scientists creating a new kind of mouse by altering the mouse's DNA to produce woolly mammoth traits.
- One experiment found that learning to drive miniature cars may reduce stress levels in rats.
- Scientists have shown that when an alligator bellows it uses resonance by placing alligators in rooms full of helium. The helium caused the bellows to change in pitch.
- Several weird experiments have been performed on plants. One unscientific experiment even led to a man named Cleve Backster claiming plants can read minds.
- The Biosphere 2 experiment attempted to test whether humans could survive long-term inside a closed environment.

- Solomon Asch's persuasion experiments demonstrated how susceptible people are to social influence.
- Several animals have been experimented on in space, including spiders and tardigrades.
- Scientists have studied how being in space affects the human body. One experiment examined identical twins, one who had spent a year in space and the other who had not.

STOP AND THINK

Surprise Me

Chapter Two describes weird experiments on animals. After reading this book, what two or three facts about these experiments did you find most surprising? Write a few sentences about each fact. Why did you find each fact surprising?

Say What?

Studying science experiments can mean learning a lot of new vocabulary. Find five words in this book you've never heard before. Use a dictionary to find out what they mean. Then write the meanings in your own words and use each word in a new sentence.

You Are There

This book discusses an experiment where rats learned to drive. Imagine you are one of the scientists. Write a letter home telling your friends what you have found. What do you notice about the rats' behavior? Be sure to add plenty of detail to your notes.

Take a Stand

Some people think that studying animals is a good way to make guesses about human beings. Other people think that animals should not be experimented on. What do you think? Is doing animal research a good use of time? Is it fair? Write a paragraph backing up your point of view.

GLOSSARY

blood pressure
a measure of the force that blood exerts on blood vessels

botanist
a scientist who studies plants

cell
the building block of all living things

communicate
to share information

conformity
behavior that is in line with social expectations

electrode
a device that attaches to the body and conducts or measures electricity

implant
to put something inside of something else

oxygen
a chemical element found in Earth's atmosphere that is used by almost all living things

vertical
positioned in an up and down direction

volume
the amount of space something occupies

ONLINE RESOURCES

To learn more about weird experiments, visit our free resource websites below.

Visit **abdocorelibrary.com** or scan this QR code for free Common Core resources for teachers and students, including vetted activities, multimedia, and booklinks, for deeper subject comprehension.

Visit **abdobooklinks.com** or scan this QR code for free additional online weblinks for further learning. These links are routinely monitored and updated to provide the most current information available.

LEARN MORE

Challoner, Jack. *Home Activity Lab: Exciting Experiments for Budding Scientists*. DK, 2024.

Kaiser, Emma. *Weird Inventions*. Abdo, 2026.

INDEX

About the Author

A. W. Buckey lives in Brooklyn, New York.